LIVE NATURAL

LIVE NATURAL

A relaxed approach to creating

healthy homes

By Alison Davin

with Cheryl Maday

Photography by Lisa Romerein

Gibbs Smith

CONTENTS

INTRODUCTION

I've always felt that our homes should be our sanctuaries. They're where we should feel safe and happy, where we recharge and relax, and where we surround ourselves with our favorite things, like art, family treasures, and meaningful mementos. I decided to pursue interior design as a way to bring this concept to life and help people create grounded, beautifully comfortable living spaces that simply feel good to inhabit.

But after being diagnosed with an autoimmune disorder fifteen years ago, I realized that the more time I spent on construction sites, the worse my symptoms became. As a new mom at the time, I wanted my family to benefit from the healthiest version of me and knew I needed to make some changes. I embarked on a several-year deep dive into my health. Leaning into the strong mind-body awareness I developed from years spent as a dancer, I connected the dots between my health and the ingredients in products I was surrounded by every day. What I uncovered transformed my entire approach to building and design.

I discovered that vapors from formaldehyde, flame retardants, and pesticides are everywhere in our homes, from building materials to mattresses. Not only are there few regulations in place to protect consumers from their potentially harmful side effects, but these hazardous ingredients are actually required by law for importation. So I made it my mission to seek out safer, chemical-free alternatives and put them into practice in my design firm, Jute.

The air we breathe and the surfaces we touch are just as significant to our health as what we eat or put on our skin. And the small everyday choices we make add up to a big impact on our climate. It's time we start looking at our environment holistically and understanding the connection between our homes, our health, and the earth. With the undeniable repercussions of climate change and growing awareness of environmental factors affecting our health, we need to start addressing the chemicals present in our homes and how to shift away from using them – without compromising on aesthetics.

Whether you're about to undergo a complete renovation of your home or are simply updating a few rooms, the conscious design choices you make can have an overwhelmingly positive effect on your health, and that of the planet. Now that we're spending more time at home than ever before, this is especially pertinent. I hope the principles I detail in this book help you create the healthiest, happiest home for you and your family – one that feels connected to nature and is made to last a lifetime.

Surround yourself with intentional,

purposeful things.

CHAPTER ONE

Light & Air

Harnessing airflow and light
to amplify your well-being

BREATHE

When it comes to air quality, we tend to think about the outside environment. This may be because of the daily index we see on our weather apps, local alerts about pollution or smog, or, more recently, forest fires.

But since most of us spend much of our time indoors, the air quality inside our homes affects us much more than what's outside. Thankfully, we can impact our indoor air quality all on our own, and this book will arm you with the knowledge to do just that. Chances are you've already made several conscious changes to improve your overall wellness, like buying organic foods, using nontoxic skincare and household products, or wearing only natural fibers. It's time for the next step in healthy living: ensuring your indoor environment is clean and that the place you call home is supporting your health.

Assess and address your indoor air quality. The first step in your home's wellness plan is to start with a baseline assessment of your indoor air quality. Think about what could be impacting it and whether you can part with the offending items. I recommend testing everything in your home, from the surfaces to your furniture and décor. You can easily do this yourself, or grab a friend for support. Once you've identified the most pressing problems, enlist friends or family (or hire a professional) to help you remove them. The good news is that once the biggest offenders are gone, it's much easier to keep your air clean going forward.

TEST

Get a VOC meter. You can find a basic, inexpensive device at your local electronics store or online. Use it everywhere to test for volatile organic compounds (VOCs) and formaldehyde, so you can evaluate and stay on top of toxicity levels in your home.

EVALUATE

Test for mold and mycotoxins. You don't need to hire professionals; just order a kit online, send in samples from various parts of your home, and determine where the issues are.

PURGE

Remove the biggest offenders. Pay close attention to mattresses, carpeting and rugs, window treatments, cabinetry, furniture, and toys. Anything sprayed with flame retardants or stain repellents or made with polyurethane, MDF, or heavy glues probably needs to go.

CIRCULATE

Check for areas that have poor ventilation. Add extractor fans to basements, attics, and any rooms that don't have free-flowing air.

REPLACE

Change the forced air filters in your heating and cooling systems, where mold and allergens tend to get trapped. Make sure the ducts are cleaned and the filters are changed regularly.

REFRESH

This one's easy: open your windows. The air outside is much cleaner than what's inside, so bring it in as frequently as possible. Cross-ventilation is always the fastest way to circulate fresh air in your home.

CLEAN

Invest in HEPA filters. Place one in every room and run continuously to remove mold, allergens, and dust from your air. You can also use specialized filters to target specific toxins.

BREATHE

When you buy new things, test everything before you bring it into the house; if it registers on your VOC meter, leave it outside to off-gas for a few days first.

A plant-filled San Francisco living room is designed for optimal breathability with solid wood floors and ceiling, plaster walls, and doors that open up to a Juliet balcony. Chairs, stool, and rug are antique.

Plan to improve your air quality over time. While you can accomplish many significant changes quickly, there can be larger issues impacting the health of your home that will require professional help. Replacing elements like walls, flooring, and windows and doors will likely need to be part of a bigger-picture project. Test everything and identify areas for improvement, then hatch a long-term plan to transform your living space into a healthier one. Keep in mind, the goal in any build or renovation should be to get your indoor air as clean as possible.

Meticulous space planning utilizing reclaimed materials added an ideal amount of cross-ventilation to this great room in Healdsburg, California. The combination of solid wood-and-steel doors creates ample airflow from multiple directions.

Windows and doors are a strategic way to harness airflow. You may think of them as sources of light, but they're also crucial in ensuring you have clean, healthy air inside your home. Ideally, you want cross-ventilation from as many different directions as possible via windows, French doors, and Dutch doors. If you have limited wall options, put in operable skylights wherever possible. One thing that may seem obvious but needs to be said: do not buy windows that you can't open easily – you will end up not using them, and that defeats the entire purpose. I suggest going to a showroom and actually operating all the windows to find the ones that work best for you. This goes for sliding doors as well, especially the heavy accordion variety.

Tall steel doors harness natural light in an indoor-outdoor dining room positioned for optimal sunset views at dinnertime.

Steel-framed doors extend all the way to the ceiling to allow light and air to permeate the space throughout the day. An antique worktable repurposed as a console adds charm.

Paint can enhance or diminish the light in each room. From a health perspective, we all need light – it elevates our mood, boosts our vitamin D levels, and regulates our circadian rhythms. Simply put, it makes us happy and enriches our lives. Because light enters your home through your windows and doors and bounces off the surfaces, the paint colors you choose can affect the quality of light in each space. Before you commit to a color scheme, observe how much time you spend in each room and how the light changes throughout the day. Pale, neutral colors enhance the sunlight and make the space feel brighter – it's why Scandinavians, who have very little daylight for much of the year, gravitate toward lighter color schemes. That said, deeper colors tend to work better in more intimate spaces that you intentionally want to be dark, like bedrooms and dens. Instead of approaching your paint colors in terms of likes and dislikes, think about how you can use them to brighten or soften the light to enhance your well-being.

A ceramic light fixture and oak chairs and table balance the cooler tones of a dining room's greige plaster walls.

Lighting should complement nature and boost your mood. I've found that people have very strong emotions when it comes to lighting, whether they're aware of them or not. My philosophy is that lighting is done best when it's sparse but strategic: you should have ample light where you need it, but not too much. Layering multiple light sources in a space is the best way to achieve this. Of course, the most energy-efficient approach is having enough natural light that you don't have to use artificial lighting; the more windows and doors in your home, the less of it you need. Take stock of your reaction to lighting — think about how the light quality in a room makes you feel — then use that to help you create the most balanced, harmonious space.

TASK

Task lights like sconces, lamps, and decorative fixtures are a must, especially if you can manipulate them via an articulated arm or shade. I recommend placing them about five feet high along the perimeter to illuminate a room in the most flattering way.

CEILING

Pendants and chandeliers should cast enough light that you don't need to turn on your recessed lighting. Use them above dining tables, kitchen islands, and entryways — anywhere it's helpful to have focused light.

RECESSED

Think of recessed lighting as "in case of emergency," like what you'd need if you lost an earring on the floor. Use it sparingly and put it on a dimmer; just because it's there doesn't mean you have to turn it on.

DIMMERS

Use these on as many fixtures as possible. Not only do dimmers give you flexibility in terms of brightness but they make your lighting more energy efficient and help your lightbulbs last longer.

REWIRING

If you find a decorative fixture you love, it's incredibly easy and inexpensive to have it rewired for higher wattage, low voltage, LED lightbulbs, or even for a different country's electrical system.

Lighting is layered to complement Mother Nature, with low-voltage LED track lights suspended from the ceiling beams, pendants over the dining area, and task lamps scattered throughout the space.

THE PUNCH LIST

Asking the right questions

Do you have a go-to filter?
My favorite brand is Rabbit Air, and I use a toxin filter, especially post construction.

What's your favorite type of door?
Dutch doors – they also function as a window and are great for adding airflow where there's little cross-ventilation.

What about glass doors?
I like French doors or sliders. They're so much easier to operate than those 3,000-pound accordion doors you see everywhere.

Do you gravitate toward a certain type of window?
I prefer those with fewer panes in solid wood or metal. The more expansive the panes, the more light comes in.

Where should skylights go?
Everywhere except the bedroom. I especially recommend one in a bathroom or above a staircase.

What's your go-to way of measuring indoor air quality?
RealTime Laboratories is an easy way to test for mold and mycotoxins. You can easily get a VOC/formaldehyde meter online.

Any rules of thumb when it comes to lighting?
Put everything on a dimmer and go for warm lightbulbs versus cool.

What's the ideal number of lights in a room?
If you don't have overhead lighting, you usually need two to six lamps to illuminate the space, depending on size.

What's your best painting tip?
I like AFM Safecoat paint. You can purchase it untinted and then take it to a paint store of your choice to have it tinted the exact color you want.

Your home should work with its natural environment,

not against it.

CHAPTER TWO

Energy & Flow

Creating harmony with the environment
and optimizing your home's wellness

FEEL

Something drew you to your home. It could have been the light, the flow, or maybe it's just in a really great location. Even if you can't put your finger on it, chances are it gave you a positive feeling, and that's something that shouldn't be ignored. It's important that you feel good in a space because when your mind is at ease, so is your body. That mindfulness helps you hone in on creating a healing environment for yourself and your family.

When it comes to the vitality of your home, there's always room for improvement. Whether you're starting from scratch or rethinking an existing structure, it's important to be intentional about your goals for a space and ensure they'll be executed in the healthiest, most harmonious way possible.

Site planning sets the relationship between your home and the land. If you're building a home from scratch, carefully consider where you want to locate it, as your structure needs to be energetically connected to its environment. Take stock of your property and get to know the landscape and the light before you begin to erect a structure. Keep in mind, you can't change your surroundings, but you can control how your house is oriented. Story poles are a helpful way to inform the views, frame moments of privacy, and harness the energy of the land. Be intentional about the sight lines and how you'll experience the indoor-outdoor flow of the space. Be self-aware enough to know how you want to live, then use that mindfulness to create the life you want.

Space planning helps you assess and improve your space. Before you begin renovating or building, you need to be clear about your priorities and what will have the biggest impact on your daily life. Before you commit to anything, take a pause and evaluate how you feel in the space. Think about what parts of your home are the most calming, which are the most energizing, which parts have the best light, and which parts you enjoy spending time in. Just because you've been inhabiting your home a certain way doesn't mean you need to use it in the same manner going forward. If you love to cook and entertain, your kitchen and living room should be in a brighter space. For better sleep, consider moving your bedrooms to a darker area. Be intentional about your goals, then reconfigure the space to suit them.

Clear sight lines allow for seamless indoor-outdoor flow, while seating areas near each door are oriented toward the light.

The dining area is maximized with a narrow yet architectural dining table and hanging console, while a large piece of art anchors the space.

Feng shui creates an energetic blueprint for your home. That energy has more of an effect on your well-being than most people realize. When you feel good in a space, you are more balanced, productive, and rested. And when you aren't, physical, relational, or financial manifestations may play out. These are the energetic tenets of feng shui. It's not a matter of hanging crystals and expecting money to fall out of the sky (although that would be nice), but rather about creating harmony in a space through balancing and enhancing the energy — and it's more instinctive than you think.

ENTRANCE

Because energy enters your space through the front door, your entrance should be wide, welcoming, and free of obstructions. Make sure it's easy to spot and not blocked by poles, trees, or clutter.

CORNERS

While squares and rectangles have better energetic boundaries for the overall floor plan of your home, pointy corners jutting at you either inside the home or from outside are not ideal.

BEAMS

Avoid low ceilings, split ceilings, and large beams directly above where you work, sit, or sleep.

LAYOUT

In seating areas, you should be able to see anyone entering a room — this is called the commanding position. In bedrooms, try to anchor your bed on a solid wall opposite the entrance.

PLUMBING

When water flows out of your home, it's considered draining energy (and money), so if possible, place your drains and sewer lines along the perimeter.

CLUTTER

Clutter interferes with the movement of energy. Always be editing your possessions. Clear out things you don't need and be purposeful with your storage.

PLANTS

Ideally you want a balance of earth, air, water, and metal elements, but plants are particularly helpful for bringing the outdoors in and creating harmony with your surroundings. Choose ones with upward, leafy growth.

A pass-through kitchen wrapped in solid wood paneling feels grounded, while purposeful storage using natural materials contains the clutter.

Energy efficiency requires thoughtful planning. With climate change being an undeniable reality, we all know that we should be lowering our fossil fuel consumption at home. Buying specific appliances and LED lightbulbs is a great start, but we need to use less energy overall, period. Because heating your home is the biggest drain on resources, addressing that should be your first goal. Orient your home to receive more natural light, especially in the winter; sunlight warms your living areas and makes you less dependent on artificial light throughout the day. Make sure your home is properly insulated so it retains heat, with wool insulation and energy-efficient windows and doors. If your local building codes permit it, plumbed radiant heat allows for consistent temperatures with no filters to keep clean. If you can add solar panels to your roof, they certainly help provide cleaner energy for the entire grid while offsetting your personal bill. Finally, small habits – like unplugging appliances when they're not being used, lowering your thermostat a couple of degrees, and using fewer lights than you truly need – can add up to a big impact for your home's carbon footprint and for the health of the planet.

Energy-efficient doors insulate heat generated by a wood-burning fireplace in the winter and let clean air flow inside in the summer.

Read labels and make healthier choices. Now that you've figured out how you want to live, it's time to implement your plans with your construction team, and that involves setting healthy guidelines every step of the process. The challenge is that there's little regulation of commonly used construction materials, and the way they're labeled can be incredibly misleading. For example, "no VOC" means that two weeks after you've used a product, certain chemicals are imperceptible in the air — not while you're applying it or immediately afterward. Instead of overwhelming yourself by trying to interpret all the marketing terminology, I recommend testing everything with your VOC meter: upon opening, upon application, and several weeks later. Decide what your limits are in terms of chemicals and communicate those clearly to your contractors. There are almost always safer alternatives out there.

SEALANTS

Since these tend to be the biggest offenders in terms of off-gassing, ask whether a material really needs to be sealed or glued, or whether there's a natural option, like fish glue.

WALLS

Long before drywall, we made walls with materials that came straight from the earth: clay, lime, plaster, stone, brick, and wood. If drywall is unavoidable, seek out less toxic brands and taping that do not contain mercury.

INSULATION

Instead of fiberglass, opt for wool or denim – they're denser, stiffer, and made with more breathable content. Wool in particular is naturally water- and fire-resistant.

PAINT

Rethink painting as a frequent way to refresh your space; even the healthiest no-VOC paints off-gas for days, if not weeks. If possible, plan to stay out of your home for a couple of weeks after you paint.

FLOORING

Rule of thumb: if a material existed before the invention of plastic, it's safe to use. Tile, hardwood, and stone pass the test; engineered wood, vinyl, laminate, and resin do not.

CARPETING

It's best to stay away from carpet in general and opt for hand-knotted area rugs instead. Carpets trap dust, allergens, and dirt, but they're even more problematic underneath, where you'll find synthetic backing, glue, and foam padding.

ROOFS

A new roof can certainly inspire sticker shock, but low-cost fabricated shingles are made with chemicals that can leech through the ceiling of your home. Clay, slate, or metal will last far longer and are safer for both you and the planet.

THE PUNCH LIST

Asking the right questions

Should you hire a feng shui consultant?
I think it's worth it. They will make you a proper bagua, or energy map, which can be kind of complicated to figure out on your own.

If you do only one thing for feng shui, what is it?
Your front door because that's how energy enters your home. Make sure it's welcoming and not blocked by anything.

Do you have any pre-move-in practices?
It never hurts to clear the energy in your home, whether by burning sage or enlisting the help of a feng shui consultant.

What's the most important thing to remove when you renovate?
MDF, OSB, particleboard, engineered wood, and fiberglass or foam insulation top my list. Use real wood where you can and replace insulation with wool or denim instead.

What's the most problematic element on the outside of your home?
You will smell a composite roof inside your home for months. Always use natural materials, even when they're outside.

Is there any safe engineered wood?
Schotten & Hansen makes a great product. But natural hardwood is always better and lasts several lifetimes.

What's your favorite chemical alternative?
Silicone is amazing; it has multiple uses as an adhesive and a sealant. Try using it to adhere countertops, baseboards, windows – anywhere a traditional epoxy is used.

What do you recommend to combat electromagnetic fields (EMFs)?
Instead of leaving Wi-Fi on all the time, try leaving it off instead and turning it on when you need to do work or to watch your favorite streaming show. It makes a big difference!

Natural materials are worth the investment,

plain and simple.

CHAPTER THREE

Warmth & Texture

Decorating with natural materials
for the health of your home

TOUCH

You can have the most architecturally beautiful house in the world, but it won't truly feel like a home until you layer in furnishings that make it approachable and comfortable. In other words, you need to decorate it. Part of this is tactile, choosing visually interesting yet warm textures that add a richness to your environment. On another level, it's adding elements that make a space feel truly personal and one of a kind. Above all, everything you choose for your home should be natural and free of chemicals so you aren't sacrificing breathability.

I personally believe that a home can never be too cozy or too customized. Here's how to decorate with the health of your home at the forefront.

Using natural fibers is the easiest way to avoid bringing chemicals into your house. Of all the items that get refreshed the most in your home, soft goods tend to be at the top of the list. Think linens, which change with the seasons or simply wear out, or throw pillows and rugs to give your home an occasional update. These items tend to be readily available, which is convenient; however, that can come at a cost. Pay careful attention to where you're buying textiles and how they're sourced. Never buy synthetics, such as polyester, which are manufactured with petroleum and will off-gas toxic chemicals in your home for their entire lifespan. Thankfully, there are many safe alternatives out there, so look for these fibers instead.

WOOL

For rugs, upholstery, bedding, and drapery, there's nothing this renewable, temperature-regulating fabric can't do. It's incredibly durable, easy to clean, and naturally fire-retardant too.

LINEN

If you've never slept on linen sheets, prepare to have your life changed. Made from flax, it's a breathable fabric that gets softer over time and lasts forever. It's also a favorite for upholstery, pillows, and windows, and block-printed linen is a great way to add pattern or color to your space.

COTTON

It's a natural choice for towels as well as bed linens, upholstery, and rugs. Make sure you look for organic cotton ideally grown in Europe – where farming standards are more strict – to limit your exposure to pesticides.

HEMP

This durable fiber stands up to wear and tear in high-traffic areas like entryways and family rooms. As a bonus, it's mildew resistant.

JUTE

I named my firm after this fiber for good reason: it's perfectly imperfect, surprisingly soft, and has amazing depth. Jute rugs add richness and warmth to a space.

Wool rugs and upholstery keep this Lake Tahoe ski cabin cozy in winter, but the lighter color scheme works in warmer weather too.

Wood products are not all made alike. When designing your home, you are likely to encounter all kinds of manufactured wood, including particleboard, medium-density fiberboard (MDF), and oriented strand board (OSB). From a health perspective alone, you want to avoid these materials because they're made with glue that contains formaldehyde and other toxic chemicals that off-gas. There's a perception that manufactured wood is more environmentally friendly because it takes less actual wood to produce, so fewer trees are cut down. That's misleading on several levels. Manufactured wood can't be sanded down and refinished, so it has a much shorter lifespan. Once you remove it from your home, it goes straight into a landfill, where it will emit carbon dioxide for years – and that's not so eco-friendly. Think long-term and invest in FSC 100% hardwood wherever possible.

A hanging, dovetailed console, wood-cased doors, an antique wooden stool, and solid hardwood floors warm up a primary bathroom.

Solid hardwood shows up in many forms in this traditional, trim-heavy home: herringbone-pattern floors, crown molding, doorjambs and casings, and wainscoting.

Flooring is one of the most impactful elements of your home's health because it covers every square foot of your living space. Your feet are constantly on it, so it comes into contact with your body in a way that your walls or countertops don't. And because heat rises, what's in your floors ends up in your air, and you don't want to breathe in any toxic chemicals. Always go for nail-down hardwood flooring; believe it or not, it's actually less expensive than engineered wood – sometimes less than half the cost per square foot. Remember: solid hardwood floors can be sanded down and refinished many times, and they'll last several lifetimes.

Plywood is the industry standard for higher-end cabinets – especially structural bases and sides – because it won't warp. However, plywood has different levels of toxicity depending on where it's manufactured; pay careful attention to its country of origin and keep in mind, this is not where you want to skimp on quality. Rule of thumb: the more white lines you see in the cross-section, the more formaldehyde has been used. For drawer boxes, I suggest dovetailed solid wood, made without glue. Because drawers use so little material, the price difference between plywood and solid wood is nominal. And since whatever you're storing inside – clothing, medicine, food – will absorb any chemicals used to make the drawer, hardwood is well worth the investment.

A fresh coat of nontoxic paint and new hardware give fresh life to hardwood built-ins and paneling – without needing to send anything to the landfill.

Choosing the right furniture is key to healthy living. As tempting as it may be to save money by purchasing mass-produced furniture, know that most of it is made with MDF, which is held together with glue and will off-gas VOCs for its lifespan. Instead, choose solid wood furniture, which is made to stand the test of time and can be refinished, repainted, or reupholstered many times over. Look for pieces made with traditional artisanal techniques like dovetail joints and mortise-and-tenon joinery, which have been used for thousands of years and don't require nails or glue. If budget is a concern, there are countless solid wood options on the secondhand market, and, as a bonus, they will have much more character than what you'd find at a mass retailer.

You can use the highest-quality FSC 100% hardwood everywhere in your house, but you'll negate its health benefits by using a regular, high-VOC stain, which will off-gas for years. Thankfully there are more and more low- and zero-VOC water-based wood stains available, and their pigments come from minerals instead of dyes. I recommend a waterborne, chemical-free, 100 percent no-VOC sealant that's formaldehyde-free and will hold in any off-gassing. This goes for cabinets, trim, baseboards, doors, or anywhere you have wood in your home.

Every piece of furniture in this room, from the custom, linen-upholstered sofa to the oversized floor lamp, is made with solid hardwood.

Antiques are the most sustainable furniture you can buy. They're built to last several lifetimes and have a nearly endless life cycle. Made the old-fashioned way from solid wood with proper joinery and without chemicals, they've already survived decades, if not hundreds of years, so they can withstand a little wear and tear. From an aesthetic perspective, they add a lot of charm and approachability to a space, which is never a bad thing. I never feel guilty about splurging on antiques, but you don't have to spend a fortune, either. Seek out hand-me-downs from family, or source your own at flea markets.

I love mixing periods and regions. Here an antique Swedish bowl atop an art nouveau dresser pairs well with a Swedish mohair chair and French mid-century rope stool.

This perfectly proportioned antique Swedish chair is reupholstered in
an indestructible wool, making it a favorite furniture piece. Not only is it
comfortable, but the design is simply timeless.

Natural stone and tile are made to last. Of the many choices you'll make while decorating your home, one of the most daunting is choosing countertops and tile; there are literally thousands of options out there. To help you narrow it down, I advise going for natural stone and tile. These materials have been used in construction for thousands of years. The Acropolis, for example, is a mixture of limestone and marble – and if it's a substance that came straight from the earth, that means it can return to the earth should you choose to rip it out, send it to a landfill, and replace it. Man-made stones such as engineered porcelain or quartz are bound by resins and glues that are harmful to breathe and take years to decompose. What's better for the planet is better for you too. Here are the healthiest choices.

MARBLE

Nothing looks more luxurious, and it's incredibly durable (again, the Acropolis). As a bonus, you can have your fabricator cut leftover stone into any shape of tile for a backsplash and save a little money in the process.

QUARTZITE

This classic stone has similar properties to marble but with a richer depth and less dramatic veining. It's so versatile I call it the linen of stone.

GRANITE

Forget the speckled countertops of the early 2000s – there's a lot of gorgeous, solid black granite out there, and I use it all the time for kitchens because it has a hard, less porous surface that's virtually indestructible. Crushed granite is also great in gardens.

SOAPSTONE

Another more uniform option with beautiful depth, soapstone is easy to keep clean, making it a solid choice for kitchens.

CLAY

This is one of the best materials for infusing color or pattern. As a bonus, so many artisans have embraced this craft that you can often find really innovative designs locally – and sourcing materials closer to home is always better for the environment.

TERRA-COTTA

This sturdy tile has an earthy quality that feels warm and cozy. With so many vendors creating fun shapes and using nontoxic glazes, it's a great way to add character to your space.

THE PUNCH LIST

Asking the right questions

Do you have a favorite type of rug?
I love Merida for custom rugs and Beni for Moroccan rugs. They both make rugs in a traditional manner without toxins. Vintage rugs are great too; just make sure you thoroughly clean them with soap and water before you bring them inside.

What are your go-to fabrics?
I love the casual feel of linen, which has more give; if you blend it with cotton, it holds its shape better. Wool is great if you want something more tailored.

What about bedding?
Linen sheets are the be-all and end-all. Seriously, they are life-changing, and they only get softer over time. Favorite brands include Libeco, Hale Mercantile, Rough Linen, and Coyuchi; some are available in organic linen.

What's your favorite material?
Wood is the number one way to make your home feel more grounded and connected to nature. The more, the better.

What's your favorite stone?
Quartzite is surprisingly affordable and comes in every sort of color and veining.

What about tile?
Reclaimed terra-cotta tile or anything handmade will have a lot more variation, which is a good thing.

What do you splurge on?
I never feel guilty about spending money on antiques. They are a non-negotiable for me.

What if you're afraid of ruining antiques?
I can understand seating, but accent tables, consoles, and stools can withstand a lot of wear and tear and work in any environment.

Longevity is the true essence of

sustainability.

CHAPTER FOUR

Ergonomics & Function

Customizing, editing, and reducing
clutter in workhorse rooms

PURPOSE

Building or renovating a home is the ultimate life makeover. It's a fresh start and an opportunity to design a better future for yourself and your family. Before you begin to think about aesthetics, take stock of your daily habits — who in your family does what, how frequently, and where — and use them to inform the design. Putting function over form is critical in rooms that have a specific purpose, like kitchens, bathrooms, and laundry rooms. In other words, these rooms will be useless if they're not usable.

Because you're in contact with the surfaces in these rooms in a way that you aren't in, say, the living room or bedroom, and especially because these spaces are where you wash your food, body, and clothes, they need to be as chemical-free as possible. And often what you leave out is more impactful than what you put in. Here's how to customize your most purposeful rooms with wellness in mind.

Simplify and strategize with thoughtful planning. As you design your kitchen or bathroom, you are probably focusing on what's going in; you're selecting materials, fixtures, and furnishings and trying to make the healthiest choices possible. But instead of fixating on elements you think you need then trying to execute them in the least toxic way, determine whether you really need them in the first place. When it comes to workhorse rooms, what you leave out is just as important as what you put in. Keep in mind that what's good for the earth is good for your home, so stick to natural materials whenever possible. Your home needs to breathe, literally and figuratively.

STORAGE

Instead of reverse engineering storage to fit everything you have, take this opportunity to assess your habits and possessions, and carve out space to hold only what you truly need.

CABINETRY

Less is more when it comes to cabinetry. The more you have, the more opportunity for toxicity. Opt for floor-to-ceiling storage instead of multicomponent systems, which have a heavier VOC load.

SURFACES

In rooms that tend to have a lot of stone and tile, be mindful of the adhesives and sealants you use, and seek out alternative solvents that come from the earth, like mineral oil.

VENTILATION

While building codes require extractor fans, windows and doors are much more efficient in clearing the air, with the added benefit of providing natural light.

FILTRATION

A full-house system can be a game changer, especially if your water is high in additives. Filtered water is not only safer to drink but better for your skin, hair, and clothes too.

Condensing storage into one big pantry cabinet allows for windows on all sides of this family kitchen and connected dining room, enabling better natural ventilation for cooking.

Kitchens are more than just where we cook our food. They've evolved into social spaces where we connect with each other over a glass of wine or an informal meal. Lately there's been a movement toward making the kitchen feel like an actual room that feels cohesive with the rest of the home versus a traditional, tucked-away space — think more cozy, less utilitarian. Instead of lining the walls with upper cabinetry, open them up with windows to increase airflow and fill the room with natural light. (I can attest that fresh air clears out any cooking odors much faster than an extractor fan.) If you love to cook, splurge on a beautiful range that allows you to take pride in nourishing your family. Add a comfy seating area or two with upholstered chairs or benches, where people can work or just spend time together. The kitchen is a place of comfort and support on many levels, and it needs to serve that purpose above all.

A pantry takes a healthy approach to storage. Back when kitchens were used primarily by staff and were more pragmatic by design, most of the food and dishware was stored in a separate butler's pantry or scullery. While most of us now do our own cooking (or plate our takeout), the idea of a dedicated kitchen storage space persists for good reason. If you don't have the square footage for a separate pantry with open shelving, allocate an entire wall to continuous floor-to-ceiling cabinetry. Not only do you get more storage space when it's not broken up into smaller drawers and cabinets, but larger-scale cabinetry uses fewer materials overall, making it less resource-intensive, with less potential for toxic elements like glue, sealants, or stains. (This is key because whatever you store inside — food, cookware, and dishes — can absorb any chemicals present.) As a bonus, it contains the clutter so you can focus on actually enjoying a clean kitchen.

The workhorse wall in this kitchen incorporates a display cabinet, a floor-to-ceiling pantry, and a concealed fridge, creating a clean wall above the range.

The most functional storage solution accommodates everything you own and determines what should be displayed and what goes behind closed doors and drawers.

Bathrooms should be your most relaxing spaces. That sense of serenity and calm you feel at a spa can also be experienced consistently in the comfort of your own home. Bathrooms are a meaningful part of our daily and nightly rituals, but they also need to be highly functional since they serve a specific hygienic purpose. In other words, the room where you get clean needs to be clean. The right approach takes your personal preferences into account and incorporates healthy practices to create the ultimate place for rejuvenation.

WCS

Creating a separate space for your toilet trumps everything else you do in this room. It's a must for privacy, feng shui, and aesthetics.

WINDOWS

Sunlight and airflow are key for mold and mildew prevention in rooms that are so heavy on plumbing, humidity, and moisture. The more windows and skylights you have, the better.

SHOWERS

Showers require tile and grout, which increases the potential for mold growth. Large-scale natural stone slabs are a way to minimize this. Avoid steam showers, which are magnets for mildew.

BATHTUBS

If you have the square footage for it, a separate soaking tub is priceless in terms of self-care indulgence and health benefits.

SINKS

Instead of having a vanity engineered to incorporate storage, I recommend something more functional, like a pedestal sink or integrated stone: that's the traditional standard.

CABINETRY

A single, streamlined floor-to-ceiling cabinet allows you to access everything from linens to toiletries and minimizes the opportunity for toxicity.

FLOORING

Unless you are a heavy dripper, I recommend hardwood in a bathroom as a stone alternative. With several coats of no-VOC polyurethane, it's just as durable as stone or tile.

A hanging, solid wood console with dovetailed drawers and an integrated stone sink maximizes storage space in a narrow bathroom while making the space feel lighter.

Closets should be treated as regular rooms. That means the same rules for using healthy materials apply here too. If your budget allows, have the same cabinetmaker who's doing your kitchen and bathroom create custom hardwood shelving and drawers for your closet. If not, stick with simple metal hanging rods and solid wood shelves. I know it's tempting, but avoid buying ready-made MDF or particleboard systems from a closet store – VOCs are not a good fit for your clothing. To determine exactly how much storage you need, take stock of everything you own: long hanging, short hanging, folded, and any sort of collections you have, like cuff links or sunglasses. I've found clients tend to use this as an opportunity to pare down their possessions and declutter their wardrobes. Think of it as designing an ideal space for your future self.

Closets should be customized to whatever they're storing – here, skis and poles in lockers with separate sections for gloves, helmets, and boots.

Laundry rooms are the kidneys of your home. Their crucial function is for cleaning your clothes and linens (and even your pets) as well as removing waste — a blast of high heat from your dryer can actually destroy allergens and dust mites. Because this is a room devoted to the act of purification — and because it's so utilitarian — I advise keeping the design light and clean: a small prep sink for hand washables, a durable stone countertop for folding and organizing, and a floor-to-ceiling hardwood cabinet for storing detergents and supplies. And with all the humidity present, mold and mildew are always a concern. For that reason, ventilation is key; the room should be located along the perimeter of your home for exhaust purposes, with operable windows or even a Dutch door for airflow.

The ideal laundry room setup has a prep sink, counter space, and extra storage, plus a game-changing window for ventilation.

THE PUNCH LIST

Asking the right questions

Why do you recommend a full-house water filtration system?
It's the best way to get filtered water in the bathroom. While there are showerheads that filter, there aren't any fixtures like that for baths or sinks.

What's your go-to kitchen sink?
A large, single-basin sink with a pull-down spray faucet generally functions best for most people.

What's your preferred way to seal stone?
Mineral oil is a totally natural, nontoxic way to do it.

Where should you use silicone?
It's great for adhering baseboards, cabinets, and the plywood underneath countertops.

What's your favorite luxury in the bathroom?
A low-energy electrical towel warmer. Plumbed towel warmers are even better, but they're hard to find – look for European vendors.

Where do you buy towels?
I love Coyuchi for organic cotton bath linens, and they have a great recycling program.

How can you design closets efficiently?
Your cabinetmaker can use leftover materials for open shelving. It's more important to use good-quality hardwood versus the particleboard you find at a closet store.

What's the easiest way to keep chemicals out of your laundry room?
Laundry detergents can be super toxic. Humidity plus chemicals is a disaster, so use the most natural formulas you can find.

Embrace the deeply restorative

power of rest.

CHAPTER FIVE

Rest & Recharge

Designing grounded environments
dedicated to sleeping and detoxing

REST

In our supercharged, always-on-the-go society, we don't emphasize rest as much as we should. The irony is that we're somehow also obsessed with the quality of our sleep, with all manner of devices and apps to track it. Rightfully so – sleep is our body's natural way of detoxing. But no number of tips or adjustments will improve your sleep quality if your body is taking in more toxins in the process. Fresh air is critical for a good night's sleep.

The rooms where you rest and recharge need to be as clean and free of chemicals as possible. Here's how to design calming, grounding spaces that prioritize health.

The primary bedroom is where your body detoxes nightly. It should also feel like a sanctuary so that you can settle into your bedtime routine free of stress. While designing a bedroom doesn't require a complex network of contractors and permits like other rooms in your home, fine-tuning the elements can be just as involved. To keep the focus on relaxation and help soothe the senses, I've harnessed the following practices to create the healthiest sleep environment.

COOL

Fresh, cool air is key to detoxing, so leave the windows open if the outside weather allows. Your ideal sleeping temperature may vary, but if you're piling on the blankets, lower is better.

CLEAN

For the cleanest possible air, invest in a high-quality HEPA filter and run it continuously. If you are going to buy only one, this is the room to use it in.

DARK

To block the light, have your curtains lined with felt or dark cotton. Avoid mass-market blackout curtains, which contain polyvinyl chloride – you don't want any off-gassing in your bedroom, especially while you're sleeping.

DIM

Set the tone for sleep with lightbulbs on the low-wattage end of the spectrum. Bonus: they won't disrupt your circadian rhythms if you turn them on in the middle of the night.

SOFT

If you suffer from allergies, remove all rugs from the bedroom, as they tend to trap dust and allergens. Otherwise, layer in comfort with a soft wool rug that hasn't been chemically treated.

SOOTHING

Essential oils aid in relaxation; try adding a few drops of lavender to your diffuser. I also recommend thieves oil, which has been used for centuries to help boost immunity and purify the air.

DISENGAGED

Turn off your Wi-Fi and phone, and use an old-school alarm clock. All of the electronic devices in your house emit low-level radiation called electromagnetic frequencies that can affect your nervous system and disturb your sleep.

The perfect sleeping conditions lean into a sparse, uncluttered space with the bed anchored on a solid wall. Our most popular request: a soothing piece of artwork to look at as you drift off.

Beds impact your sleep quality more than anything else. But when it comes to designing them, there's not a one-size-fits-all approach. To customize yours in the way that works best for you, think about how you use your bed and how it can most effectively support how you sleep. Keep in mind that because there are so many layers of bedding, there are more opportunities for off-gassing. Rule of thumb: for the most grounding sleep, always choose materials that came from the earth, not from the factory. Here are all the elements to consider when making your bed healthy.

BED

For the best support and fewest toxins, a solid hardwood bed frame with a slatted base is ideal. If you gravitate toward upholstered headboards, choose a natural, breathable fabric like wool, cotton, or linen.

MATTRESS

Natural latex or wool mattresses are breathable, hypoallergenic, and biodegradable. As a bonus, these organic materials can last up to twenty years — much longer than the conventional, chemical-heavy options found at a mattress store.

TOPPER

For an added layer of comfort, a topper can make your bed extra cozy and help your mattress last longer. I recommend wool versus down fill, as it's naturally intuitive, antimicrobial, and flame retardant.

BEDDING

Always choose organic fibers, and pay particular attention to country of origin; the safest textiles come from Europe via air, which eliminates the need for pesticides in shipping.

BLANKETS

While not for everyone, weighted blankets can calm your nervous system and help you reach REM sleep faster. If glass balls aren't your thing, you can achieve a similar effect by piling on several regular blankets.

PILLOWS

The cleanest option is 100 percent organic natural latex with a cotton cover. Latex is antimicrobial and resistant to mildew and dust mites, making it great for anyone with allergies — and it's more durable than down fill.

Guest rooms should feel welcoming yet private. To help visitors feel as comfortable as possible in your home, the same principles apply here as in your other bedrooms – cool temperature, cozy materials, clean air – with two notable distinctions. First, it's a good idea to provide extra storage so your guests can put away their things and not feel like they need to live out of a suitcase for the duration of their stay. An antique wardrobe or dresser is a whimsical yet functional way to do this. The other is that, if possible, the guest room should be removed from the rest of the bedrooms for privacy; a separate wing is ideal, a separate floor is even better, and a separate accessory dwelling unit (ADU) is a game changer, if you have the budget and space for one.

This Cabo San Lucas guest cottage feels like a true escape, layered with local textiles and ample storage options for visitors.

Sometimes an amazing view is all the décor you need to make your space feel like a retreat. This lake-facing bedroom is oriented to emphasize its serene focal point.

Kids' rooms need to flex as the children grow. The place where your little ones get much-needed rest is also where they indulge their favorite activities and pursue their passions. The challenge is that much of the décor geared toward children is filled with chemicals that do more harm than good — think PVC blackout curtains to help them sleep or stain-resistant synthetic fibers to make cleaning up easier. Kids' developing bodies need fresh, clean air just as much as you do, so opt for organic, nontoxic materials whenever possible. Thankfully, there are many ways to create a space that feels personal and playful without sacrificing wellness.

BEDS

Custom hardwood bunk beds can serve as playtime nooks and host sleepovers when the kids are older. Otherwise, daybeds with trundles are popular for sleepovers and extra guests.

RUGS

Bright colors and a fun pattern — even a bespoke one the kids can help design — can really spruce up the room. Because kids are on the floor a lot, a rug in a durable yet low-maintenance natural fiber like wool is a must.

WALLS

Painting stripes or a custom mural are ways to infuse color. But if you have your heart set on wallpaper, look for those printed on no-VOC paper with water-based ink.

LIGHTING

Get creative with sconces or overhead fixtures, like a glamorous princess chandelier or a lantern that shoots stars. Because these are chiefly metal or glass, they tend to be made with safer materials.

STORAGE

Kids love to display their things, and as they grow and develop, their needs change. Custom hardwood shelving can be adjusted as smaller, softer toys give way to bigger projects like LEGOs.

PLAY

Teepees and swings are popular if space allows; interactive elements can be hung on walls — everything from chalkboards, pin boards, and maps to climbing walls.

An early-teens redecoration of your kid's room can introduce a bigger bed, fun patterned rugs and pillows, and statement artwork into their more grown-up space.

Home gyms encourage healthy habits. We all know the benefits of regular exercise, and I've found it's much easier – not to mention more motivating – to work out in a beautiful space in the comfort of your own home. The design doesn't need to be complicated; wood floors absorb impact and can be easily cleaned, and ample windows or French doors are ideal for airflow, especially when you're breathing heavily and releasing toxins. And while it may be tempting to build your own mini Equinox, the most purposeful space will be one tailored to how you prefer to exercise – weights, Pilates, Peloton, etc. I recommend sourcing gently used equipment that's already off-gassed, as exercise gear tends to be heavy on plastic for durability.

A fitness sanctuary can look like any other room – hardwood floors, linen drapery, glass doors – just with a Pilates Reformer and stylish storage for free weights.

THE PUNCH LIST

Asking the right questions

What are your favorite bedding resources?
Hale Mercantile, Sferra, and Libeco all have great organic linens for the bed and bath.

Where do you find thieves oil?
I buy mine from Young Living; other brands sell something similar, called a "medieval blend."

Do you use a humidifier?
No, and I don't recommend them because they can foster mold.

Do you use a different air purifier in the bedroom?
Molecule air filters are small and can fit in tight spaces, like kids' bedrooms.

Where do you find nontoxic furnishings for kids?
European Sleep Works makes a natural latex mattress for kids that's very affordable. There are many solid wood beds and cribs out there too.

What's the most important thing to know about kids' rooms?
Avoid buying gimmicky things from chain stores that have been sprayed with flame retardants – they do more harm than good.

Why should you avoid metal in your bed?
If you're sensitive to EMFs, the metal could act like an antenna and make it worse.

What's your favorite bedroom decorating trick?
I like to use artwork to decorate the walls versus wallpaper, which involves a lot of chemicals, like glue.

Make space for joy in your

home.

CHAPTER SIX

Welcoming & Entertaining

Inviting guests into clean,
thoughtfully designed spaces

WELCOME

Your home's main living area might be an open-concept great room or a series of smaller rooms, but no matter how it's laid out or what you call it, you probably spend most of your waking hours there. This space needs to work for multiple purposes as well, from entertaining guests to hanging out and relaxing with family. Not only should it feel comfortable, it should also be designed with healthy, nontoxic materials.

Every room should have a mix of new and old, customized and character-filled. Here's what to keep in mind when designing your living and dining spaces.

Upholstery can be customized without chemicals. Living rooms tend to be where most of the upholstered furniture in your home is found, and where there's upholstery, there's often off-gassing, especially if you have man-made fabrics, foam, fabric retardants, or stain-resistance treatments – all of which are prevalent in items purchased at chain stores. Commissioning custom-made pieces or reupholstering antiques, hand-me-downs, or furniture you already own are the most ideal ways to avoid chemicals that will off-gas, but many retailers do stock mindfully made furniture. Here's what to look for when you're reading labels.

FRAMES

Look for solid hardwood frames, made properly with dovetail joints versus glue. Avoid plywood and MDF frames, which contain formaldehyde and will off-gas for years.

FILL

Down fill is a soft, sustainable option, but getting the density right can be tricky. For firmer cushioning, opt for plant-based foam, latex, wool, or any of those wrapped with down.

FABRIC

When durability is a concern, go for linen, cotton, hemp, wool, or a blend. As a bonus, you can remove the cushion covers and throw them in the washing machine. Avoid any stain-resistant treatment, which uses PFAS (forever chemicals like Teflon and Scotchgard).

TRIM

Choose hardwood over MDF. Any visible wood should be finished in a nontoxic stain. Metal legs are also a good option.

PILLOWS

Repurpose the decorative down-filled pillows you likely already have; you can source your own untreated fabric and have new covers custom made at your local dry cleaner.

THROWS

These always make your seating feel extra cozy and finished. My go-tos are alpaca or wool-alpaca blends, which last the longest and don't pill.

Leather, wool, and linen are naturally reliable options for upholstery. If durability is a concern, dark colors are more forgiving in terms of spills, stains, and general wear and tear.

Televisions don't have to be hidden. Technology has become such a part of our lives that no one hides it anymore. Twenty years ago, when TVs were huge, concealing them behind a cabinet became a fad. Today, we have frame TVs so thin and lightweight they can be hung on the wall like a painting. The problem with trying to cover up TVs is that technology moves so fast, the pieces we construct to house them will no longer be the right size in a few years and they'll end up in a landfill. The faster technology evolves, the more waste we create. So opt out of that cycle and display your TV proudly.

Thanks to thoughtfully considered storage and seating, this media room feels cohesive with the rest of the home.

Vintage furnishings lower your carbon footprint. Buying antique or vintage furniture is one of the greenest choices you can make while decorating your home. It keeps items out of the landfill, prevents more trees from being cut down, and avoids all of the harmful manufacturing and shipping processes involved in producing new furniture. As a bonus, it's my favorite way to make a space feel more personal and unique. I think every room should have a mix of new and old, so try layering in some charm with these pieces.

SEATING

There are countless vintage options on the market that can easily be refinished and reupholstered in the nontoxic materials of your choice.

CHAIRS

Since these don't usually withstand a lot of wear and tear, they tend to be in good supply. Look for hardwood frames, nontoxic interior fill, and upholstery in a breathable, natural fabric.

TABLES

In solid wood, these are built to last and can be sanded and refinished many times over with a water-based, non-VOC stain.

STORAGE

With so many options out there in terms of credenzas, buffets, bookcases, and cabinets, it's almost ridiculous to buy something brand new.

RUGS

New rugs can off-gas more than anything else in your home; a rug that's already done so for years is a safer bet. These are almost always wool, but jute, cotton, or sisal are also ideal.

LIGHTING

Metal chandeliers, pendant lights, and sconces can last for hundreds of years, and rewiring them for energy-efficient LED bulbs is easier than you'd expect.

TABLETOPS

If you don't have family heirlooms or hand-me-downs, these can easily be found at vintage stores, flea markets, or auction sites online – often at very affordable prices.

Homes should always have a balance of new and old. Preserving original architectural details like windows and beams — and layering in vintage rugs and mirrors — helps maintain a space's charm.

Bars lend themselves to natural materials. They tend to be wood- and stone-heavy in terms of countertops, backsplash, cabinetry, and storage, and I've found that most clients don't hesitate to go for high-end natural materials for them. There's a certain timelessness to this space that lends itself to a big investment — and one that really makes a statement in terms of welcoming guests into your home. I tend to tailor them to individual preferences — wine fridges, beer drawers or taps, locked cabinets for spirits — and make them feel like beautifully cultivated places to socialize and indulge.

Your bar space should be personalized for how you like to entertain — in this case, with storage to display an impressive collection of wine.

In a Cabo San Lucas dining room oriented to maximize the views, the all-wood bar and serving station is strategically tucked away into a functional wall niche.

The dining room should prioritize function over form. Since this is a room where you consume food – and tend to linger – the materials you use should, above all, support the wellness of your guests. To design a healthy table, consider three main points: who will be in the room, how long they'll be hanging out there, and how often it will be used. The answers will inform everything from the size of the table itself to the comfort level of the chairs to the lighting design – and the healthy decisions you make.

TABLES

A custom design is the best way to accommodate your guests. New or repurposed hardwood tabletops are worth the investment, although natural stone is a solid alternative. The base can be wood or metal.

CHAIRS

Use upholstery sparingly – the more you have, the greater potential for off-gassing. Metal, solid wood with caning, or semi-upholstered with a natural fiber or leather is a safe bet; vintage is even safer.

LIGHTING

Instead of recessed lighting, go for a decorative fixture like a pendant or a chandelier to anchor the space and set the tone. Sconces or a table lamp on a buffet also cast a soft illumination.

STORAGE

Considering that what you store inside your credenza, buffet, or console absorbs the materials it's made from, I recommend solid wood with a nontoxic stain or ideally a vintage piece.

DETAILS

Invest in adding arches, ceiling beams, a herringbone wood or tile floor, or something that makes the room feel more architecturally significant and special.

In a room that can be relegated to special occasions, a gorgeous wood grain and architectural metal legs make this dining table look decorative even without place settings.

Artwork is good for your mental and emotional health. It can elevate your mood, calm your feelings, and simply improve the quality of your life. To start your collection, visit local art fairs to find artists you like – the galleries that represent them can help you source more work that appeals to you. If your budget allows for only smaller pieces, get creative with matting and framing to make a piece appear more substantial. You can also blow up your own photos into large-scale prints. Make sure you use solid wood framing – it's the industry standard for fine art, and a good-quality custom frame truly makes a piece shine. Find out where your gallery gets their pieces framed, and take yours there. Hang your art where you can enjoy it: think entertaining areas like the dining room, pass-through spaces like hallways and landings, and anywhere people hang out.

Artwork placed strategically to delineate a space can serve as a conversation piece as well as anchor writing and dining tables.

THE PUNCH LIST

Asking the right questions

Where do you source upholstered furniture?
I look for mindfully made American brands like Lee Industries and Cisco Home.

What should people know about reupholstery?
It's not going to save you money; the important thing is that it's decreasing waste, saving something you like, and giving it new life with better materials.

What should you always avoid with upholstery?
Never add stain-resistant treatment to anything, even if it has the word "eco" in it.

How can you minimize EMFs in living areas?
Use cables instead of running everything on Wi-Fi. The bonus is that it gives you a more stable connection.

What's something to consider when buying vintage furniture?
Try to buy yours locally instead of shipping it across the country, which creates a huge carbon footprint.

How do you maintain wood furniture without chemicals?
People have used mineral wax and steel wool for hundreds of years, and that's still the gold standard today.

What's something people don't expect when it comes to dining rooms?
They tend to be one of the most expensive rooms in your home because of all the furniture – the chairs especially can add up.

What's the best way to source art?
Art fairs happen in every city and in lots of small towns too. They're the best place to discover artists you like.

Your home is more than the space

inside its walls.

CHAPTER SEVEN

Outdoor Living

Borrowing from the earth to
create healthy outside areas

GROUND

The essence of designing with natural elements is a seamlessness
between indoors and outdoors: think a lack of doors, a continuous
flow of air, a blending into the natural landscape, and an overall
feeling of wellness that can only come from nature. While only
a select (and lucky) few of us live in a climate that allows for that
experience year-round, there are certainly tenets of outdoor
living that you can incorporate into your own home. It's a matter
of utilizing materials that come straight from the earth that can be
reused or repurposed – so that the transition not only looks natural
but feels natural too.

Think of it as borrowing from the earth and giving back when
you're done. Here's how to design beyond the walls of your home
and integrate your outdoor environments with wellness in mind.

Indoor-outdoor flow should feel effortless. Instead of thinking of your outdoor space as a separate entity, consider it an extension of your living space. An easy place to start is by anchoring an area to the side of your home so that it's literally just outside your door. The more informal, the better — all you need is somewhere to carve out a moment that can easily become part of your daily routine. The more time you're able to enjoy outdoors, the better your quality of life.

This frequently used outdoor dining area is anchored on a retaining wall and defined with columns and light fixtures.

Natural materials are good indoors and even better outdoors. There are some subtleties to designing an outdoor space versus indoor. For one, you want to move away from the light outside, rather than toward it as you would inside. And you do need to keep weather-resistance in mind. But in general, the practices you apply indoors should be used outdoors — especially since the furnishings you place outside can affect the greater atmosphere. Instead of plastic or pressure-treated wood, choose materials that come from the earth and look even more at home in their natural environment. Here are the healthiest options for air quality.

HARDWOODS

For wooden furniture and decks that weather well, teak and cedar are the gold standard. Ipe and redwood are also solid choices for decking.

WOVENS

Rattan or wicker furniture is a great way to add texture to a more covered area. Reed coverings are inexpensive and make great awnings, as they let light filter through.

METAL

For an ultra-durable option, go for aluminum, stainless steel, or any metal that's been treated for outdoor use. I particularly love French bistro chairs and tables for outdoor dining, as they're lightweight and can easily be moved around.

LAVA STONE

Lava stone, bluestone, and limestone are go-tos for anchoring or delineating an area. As a bonus, they will hold up to heavy wear and tear.

CONCRETE

Basically a mixture of stone, sand, and water, this low-maintenance material gets stronger over time and is naturally resistant to erosion.

TILE

Hand-painted terra-cotta tiles are a chic way to define a space. I use them frequently in outdoor dining areas and around pools.

Outdoor fabrics should be used sparingly. In order to stand up to the elements and be easily cleaned, most have a plastic component to them. Consider their functionality; they should feel soft to the touch and add a layer of coziness to your space – for example, removable custom cushions on teak dining table seating. Look for a mix of linen or other natural fibers with a touch of polyester for durability.

Hanging back cushions in Everywhere Linen add just the right amount of padding to built-in wood benches with deep seating.

This California home strikes the right balance outdoors with furniture that's heavier on natural hardwood like teak while integrating into the home's hardscape of wood, plaster, and limestone pavers.

Outdoor lighting sets the tone and anchors your space. You can also have a little fun with it: think pendant lights, whimsical sconces, decorative lanterns, and string lights. Always buy lighting that's outdoor safe; anything too precious will get battered by the elements. Powder-coated bronze, for example, weathers beautifully. For navigational purposes, in-ground LED lighting in the hardscaping is the way to go. As a rule of thumb, treat outdoor lighting as you would indoor: it should cast a flattering glow and complement nature, not overwhelm it.

A single Spanish-style statement sconce cased in glass adds character and illuminates a large outdoor area.

Outdoor rooms should mirror your indoor living space. Unless you live in an industrial loft, the interior of your home isn't a vast space with a bunch of furniture strewn about; it's a series of smaller, purposeful rooms. To create a similar sense of intimacy, I suggest carving out distinct areas in your outdoor space. It doesn't matter if you are working with acres of land or a tiny courtyard; it's simply a matter of designating several different zones that feel cozy and distinct.

KITCHEN

The grill is the main event, although outdoor pizza ovens are gaining in popularity. It's helpful to include a countertop with a small prep sink and a fridge underneath, plus a few lower cabinets and drawers for storage.

BAR

Often integrated with the outdoor kitchen, a bar can also serve as a stand-alone area that feels like a separate destination. Comfy barstools are key, and I'll often include a beer tap and wine fridge for easy access.

DINING

This can be an informal, built-in banquette tucked along the side of your house or a more formal stone or wood dining table with a pendant light overhead and chairs or benches. Overhead coverage is key so you're not blinded by the sun while eating.

LIVING

Since this space is best suited to conversation, I like to outfit the area with an outdoor sofa or two, a low cocktail table, and a couple of chairs. Layer in some cushions covered in weather-resistant fabric for an extra bit of coziness.

LOUNGE

Furnished with a daybed or chaise lounges, think of this as a poolside spot for catching a bit of sun or a shaded area for curling up with a good book.

FIRE

A fireplace or firepit surrounded by Adirondack chairs or built-in seating is often the area that gets the most year-round use. The latter is especially easy to do since there are so many options that don't require running a gas line across your yard.

A multipurpose outdoor space feels like a natural extension of the living area just outside the home, while a simple, shaded swing takes advantage of the landscape's natural cover.

Soil is everything when it comes to your yard. The key to gardening without chemicals or pesticides is improving the quality of your soil. Healthy soil is full of microorganisms that protect plants and nutrients that plants need to grow; healthy plants are less vulnerable to pests (see how that works?). If you can afford to overhaul your garden and incorporate biodynamic soil, I highly recommend it – it's more fertile, balanced, and adaptive. Your plants will grow like crazy, the entire ecosystem of your yard will change, and the results will be better for the planet as a whole.

Choose the right landscaping for your climate and soil by planting what's native to your area. Keep in mind that precipitation, sunlight, extreme temperatures or wind, and existing vegetation can affect what you plant. In order to grow a healthy, thriving garden, I recommend visiting a local nursery that specializes in plants native to your area; they can help you select the best options. Keep in mind that while it can be challenging to find nurseries with entirely pesticide-free plants, you can readily seek out varieties with no added pesticides. Paired with biodynamic soil, it's a recipe for a healthier outdoor environment.

Landscaping with native plants and ground cover appropriate to your climate ensures that they'll thrive in your yard.

THE PUNCH LIST

Asking the right questions

Should you use different materials outdoors?
Teak and cedar are the best woods for outside, but otherwise anything that's good indoors, like stone, is even better outdoors.

What about dishes and glassware?
I buy inexpensive glass and earthenware. You don't want to use plastic or melamine, especially in the sun.

How do you make sure you use your outdoor living areas?
A seating area very close to your home, like a deck or patio, will get you outside more frequently without having to travel too far.

How can you avoid off-gassing outdoors?
Use fabrics very sparingly and be especially careful of anything marketed as "eco."

What makes artificial grass so bad?
Aside from the fact that it's made of plastic, you have to install it on an asphalt base that's even more toxic.

What's your preferred type of fencing?
I'm a fan of hedges versus fences. Anytime you can use plants versus resources, it's helpful.

What's your stance on gardening?
Plant what's native to your area, because that's what's best for your environment, and as a bonus, you won't exhaust yourself trying to make it grow.

Should you ever use pesticides?
Never, under any circumstances. Just no.

ABOUT

Alison Davin is the founder of the interior design firm Jute and an expert in nontoxic building and decorating. With over fifteen years of experience, Ali has honed a health-conscious, chemical-free approach to construction without sacrificing design aesthetic. Showcasing natural materials, artisanal techniques, and one-of-a-kind pieces, her work has been featured in *Architectural Digest*, *Elle Decoration*, and *Luxe*, and she launched a bespoke product line in 2020. She currently resides in Sausalito, California, where she renovated her home without chemicals.

Lisa Romerein is a renowned photographer specializing in architecture, interiors, gardens, and food. Her work has appeared in over twenty books and countless magazine, editorial, and commercial campaigns. A native of Seattle, she grew up with the natural world as her first and most influential creative teacher. Her intuitive handling of light and composition reflect her respect for the simple elegance and natural beauty of life. She resides in Santa Monica, California, nestled between the ocean and mountains, savoring the marine-layer days that remind her of the Northwest.

Cheryl Maday is the writer behind *Second Nature*, the Jute blog. As an editorial director, she has shaped sustainability standards, product messaging, and advertising campaigns for global luxury fashion and beauty brands. Diagnosed with an autoimmune disorder as a teenager, Cheryl is a proponent of blending Western medicine with alternative healing modalities like acupuncture, herbs, and nutrition. She lives in an antiques-filled Victorian in San Francisco.

ACKNOWLEDGMENTS

Thank you to Rowan. I am forever grateful for your patience as we have worked on this book and for all of your guidance on art direction. | To Patrick for teaching me about building in a way only a contractor could and for building and rebuilding so many spaces till they were perfect. | To Bekah for working with me for over a decade and for your endless support of my nonstop thinking up of projects and caring as much as I do. | To Liddy for your support and cheerleading all these years and for helping make the book beautiful. | To Lisa for creating beautiful imagery and being Rowan's favorite photographer. | To Cheryl for writing with me for years and for making kind of scary topics seem so approachable. | To Joy for your wisdom and support in navigating the book process. | And, lastly, to Madge for being so enthusiastic about our book and being a delight to work with.

First Edition
28 27 26 25 24   5 4 3 2

Text © 2024 Alison Davin
Photographs © 2024 Lisa Romerein
Author portraits by Thomas Kuoh, pages 8 and 232

Published by
Gibbs Smith
P.O. Box 667
Layton, Utah 84041

1.800.835.4993 orders
www.gibbs-smith.com

Book design by Bekah Fletcher and Liddy Walseth

Library of Congress Control Number: 2023945639
ISBN: 978-1-4236-6582-3

Printed in China using FSC® Certified materials

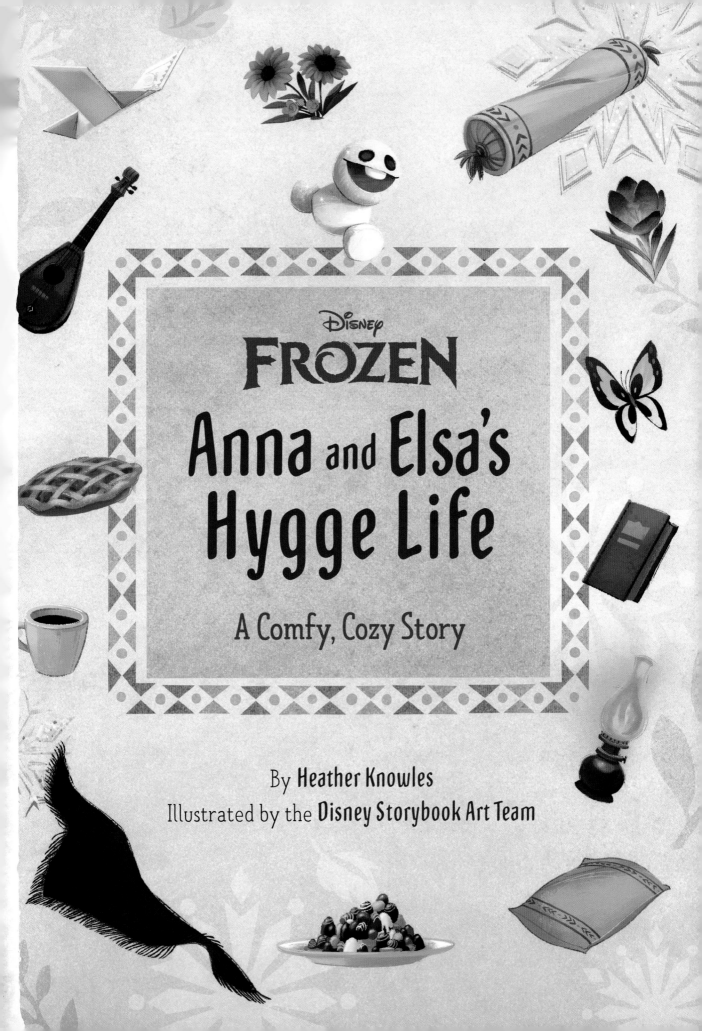

Disney
FROZEN
Anna and Elsa's Hygge Life

A Comfy, Cozy Story

By **Heather Knowles**
Illustrated by the **Disney Storybook Art Team**

It was time for **Olaf's weekly trip to the library**. As usual, after **returning the books** he had read, the first thing he did was greet all the others.

"Good afternoon, books. Which one of you should I read today?" Olaf said, gazing up at the tall shelves.

The little snowman climbed up high and looked at every book. "I've read it. Read it. Read it. Wait . . . **what's this**?" Olaf grabbed one with a blue cover. He couldn't quite pronounce the title, *Hygge*, but it looked like one of his favorite words. "Could this book be about hugs?"

He took the book to his **favorite reading nook** and opened it to the first page. But before he could start reading, Oddvar, the librarian, announced that the library was **closing** for the day.

Olaf checked out a new stack of books and headed home. He was so excited to begin reading **an entire book about hugs** that he flipped the book open as he entered the castle courtyard.

"'**Hygge** is all about being **comfortable and cozy**.
It is something you can share with family and friends or
experience by yourself,'" he read.
"How do you give yourself warm hugs?"
Olaf said out loud. "I'll have to ask Anna and Elsa."

Later that evening, Olaf shared his book with his friends.
"It's a book about hugs! See? It says it right there on the
cover. Although I think someone spelled *hug* wrong."

Elsa smiled. "That's not *hug*, Olaf, it's *hygge*. It's the feeling of **warmth and contentment** that you get on the inside when you do certain things. But some people think that the word *hygge* comes from *hug*."

"**Huge-got-what-now?**" Olaf asked.

"**Hue-guh,**" Anna said slowly. "I get a **hyggeligt** feeling whenever I put on big fuzzy socks."

"I always get a **sense of hygge** when I buy things for people that I know they will **love**," Kristoff said. "Like when I gave Anna a **box of chocolates** the other day."

Elsa's eyes widened. "Do you have any left?" she whispered to her sister.

"I just might," Anna answered.

"To know Kristoff thought of me and bought me the chocolates **just because he loves me** filled me with such happiness. Even after I ate too many of them and my stomach was a bit upset, I was still **hyggeligt**, or **filled with contentment**, for the rest of the day," Anna said, laughing.

"For me, my earliest memory of experiencing hygge was **spending time with Mother and Father**."

"I loved listening to their stories, and they enjoyed hearing our stories, too," Anna said. "The **joy** we shared in those moments together as a family was hygge."

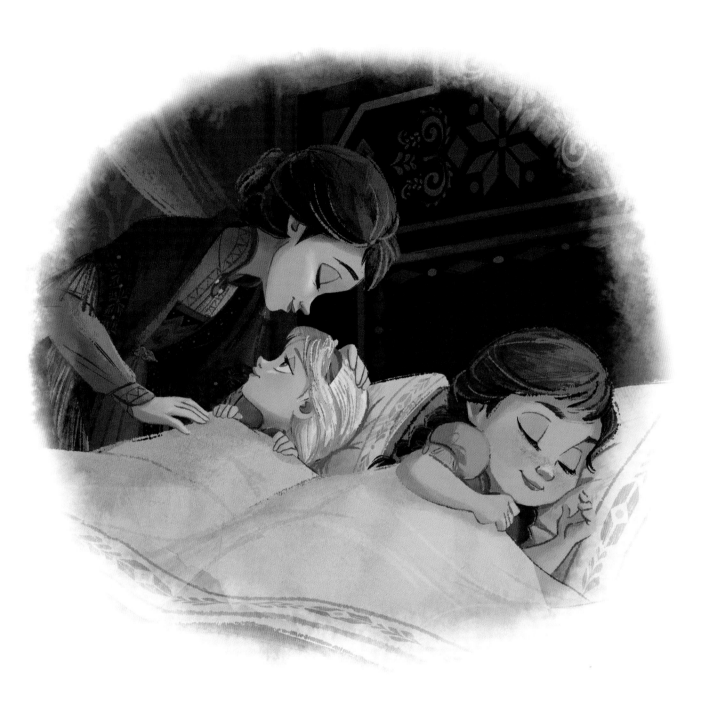

"And listening to Mother **sing** always made me feel warm and content," Elsa said. "To this day, **wearing her shawl** or **singing the same songs** brings back that hyggeligt feeling."

"**Singing** is part of hygge for me, too," Kristoff said. "Sven and I used to sing a lot together in the barn before we met you guys. That and the **smell of hay**, the **crunch of carrots**, and the **jingling of reindeer bells** all make me relaxed and happy."

"And I love when we sing with your **troll family**," Anna said. "Since the moment I first met them, I've felt nothing but **comfortable and welcomed**. Being with them always makes me feel hyggeligt."

"I felt **warm and excited** when I met them, too," said Olaf. "I just didn't know those feelings had such a **special** name."

19

Olaf continued to think about examples of hygge.
He remembered the first time he met Sven.

"When he tried to **kiss my nose**, I felt **giggly and happy**," said Olaf.

"That's hygge!" said Kristoff.

"I get the best **hyggeligt feeling** when Marshmallow hugs me. Do you think that's why I love **warm hugs** so much?" Olaf asked.

"I wouldn't be surprised if that was **one of the reasons**," Anna said.

"Actually, I love just spending time with
my **little brothers**, whether they are **awake
or asleep**," Olaf said. "That's hygge, too, right?"

"It sure is!" Elsa said. "Just like I love being with all of you whether we are in the castle **in front of a fire** or in the forest **under the stars**, or even when we **aren't doing anything at all**."

"We've shared hyggeligt moments **playing games** and **eating snacks**."

"Can hygge also be the
feeling you get when you **draw
pictures of your family**?"
"**Absolutely!**" Anna said.

"How about **reading books to children** during story time at the library? That must be hygge!" said Olaf.

"Can it also be **cake**, and **a picnic**, and **candles**, and **honey**, and **flowers**, and **hot chocolate**?" Olaf asked.

"It is for me!" Elsa said with a laugh.
"And for me, too!" Anna agreed.

"I've always loved **summer days**," said Olaf. "But now I think there's **something else** that I love even more."

"Let me guess," said Anna. **"Could it be . . ."**

"HYGGE!" everyone exclaimed together.
"And for me, hygge means **spending time with all of you . . . my best friends . . . my family,**" Olaf said.